Redefining
JOY
IN THE LAST DAYS

Redefining JOY

IN THE LAST DAYS

CHRIS STEWART

DESERET
BOOK

SALT LAKE CITY, UTAH

Library of Congress Cataloging-in-Publication Data
Stewart, Chris, 1960–
    Redefining joy in the last days / Chris Stewart.
        p. cm.
    ISBN 978-1-60641-035-6 (hardbound : alk. paper)
    1. Happiness—Religious aspects—Church of Jesus Christ of Latter-day Saints. I. Title.
    BX8643.H35S74 2009
    248.4′89332—dc22   2008046938

Printed in the United States of America
R. R. Donnelley, Crawfordsville, Indiana

10 9 8 7 6 5 4 3 2 1

S OME YEARS AGO, when I was in the Air Force, I found myself flying from a tiny British base in the Indian Ocean. I'd been away from home for many weeks and was very anxious to get back to my wife and children. Unfortunately, we had mechanical issues with our aircraft that required us to divert into the Philippines. Late in the afternoon, we arrived at Osan Air Force Base with only a short announcement that we were coming. Because of this, the base had no officers quarters to offer us, and so they sent us downtown.

I remember stepping out of the taxi at one of the downtown hotels. It was a beautiful building: chrome and glass, thick carpet, and beautiful woodwork. But as I made my way across the crowded sidewalk, I couldn't help but notice a high, chain-link fence stretched across a blocked-off street that ran immediately behind the hotel.

I went into the fine lobby, registered, agreed to meet the rest of the crew for dinner, and followed a bellboy to my room. Having been up since early in the morning (very early, as in some absurd 2:00 A.M. takeoff time), I was very tired as I entered the room and threw my bags on the bed. To be honest, at this time I was in a foul mood. I was frustrated that we'd spent so much time messing with a broken aircraft, frustrated that I was thirsty but afraid to drink the water, frustrated that I had to spend another night away from home. The bed looked lumpy. The room had bugs, of course—everything in the Philippines had bugs. I knew the only American shows I'd be able to watch on the television would be old reruns of *The Brady Bunch*. I was out of gum. I had broken a lace in my boot. My head was starting to pound.

My list of reasons for being in a bad mood was long and full.

Hoping for a quick nap, I went to the window to pull the curtains closed. My window happened to be at the back of the hotel on the second floor. Looking down, I saw the reason for the fence, for there behind the hotel was an open aqueduct with several terraced levels upon which hundreds of people had built a shanty camp. Families were living all along the sides of the canal—some in cardboard houses, some in tents, many in the open. For a long time I stood by the window in my air-conditioned room, tired but not hungry, with a headache but otherwise healthy, and very happy that I was going home. Home to the United States, land of freedom and plenty. Home to a wife and family who were fortunate enough not to live in a ditch and who had never once in their lives gone hungry. Home to more blessings than I could even count.

Standing by the window, I watched a young mother as she washed her daughter's face and hair with the filthy water that was rushing from a pipe feeding into the canal. The scene touched me deeply. I can remember it very clearly, even through the years.

And as I watched this young family, hungry, dirty, homeless, and certainly nearly hopeless, I suddenly felt so ashamed of my selfishness.

I learned a lesson that day about feeling sorry for myself.

I think of that experience from time to time, especially when, once again, I find myself feeling a little down. Sometimes I have to wonder if I learned the lesson well enough. Do I appreciate the blessings I've been given? Or do I forget sometimes—I guess we all do—the attitude and perspectives it takes to live a happy and joyful life?

Do We Remember Why We're Here?

I'D LIKE TO ASK A QUESTION. At the risk of stating what might seem too obvious, I'd like to ask you to consider: "What is the purpose of our life here on earth?"

Think about that for a moment.

Why are we here?

When I was a missionary, we used to ask this question as part of the missionary discussions. These are the answers that we used to teach, best as I can remember:

First, we came to gain a body.
We also came to gain experience.
Third, we came to prove ourselves.
And finally, we came to develop faith.

Have I forgotten anything? I think we got it pretty close. Those are the reasons we are here—and they're good reasons. Can't argue with much of this.

Now, let me ask just a slightly different question. In doing so, I hope to expand our perspective, maybe help us look at the much bigger picture, to see beyond this life and the things that we experience here. After all, we know that in the whole scheme of things this life is but a single drop in the ocean. As important as it is, this life is just a single phase in a much larger and much grander and much more majestic plan.

So then, looking at the bigger picture, let me ask: What is the purpose of our existence? Why do we exist?

Maybe we don't know every answer to that question, but we know at least one, for the scriptures tell us: "Men are, that they might have joy" (2 Nephi 2:25).

I really believe that.

I really believe, at its essence, that this is the reason we exist.

The problem is, of course, there are so many obstacles placed in our way. I hate that! So many challenges are placed in what we hoped would be a flower-strewn path of unending happiness. *How could I possibly be happy when I have to live with ...* I don't know, you fill in the blank. *I work fifty-hour weeks, I'm supposed to be stressed. The stock market has collapsed, taking my retirement fund with it. My husband hasn't had a raise in five years. I've got to lose twenty pounds. My kids have all grown up and are going to move away.* Hold on, here's a bad one: *All of my kids have grown up, but are going to move back home!*

I mean, come on, the list of reasons we can't be happy right now is *really, really* long.

And some of these reasons are significant: *My mom is sick. I want to get married. I lost a child. I'm losing a child.* You'll notice that the most significant challenges we encounter usually center on the relationships in our lives. Those of us who have cried over our children, our marriages, our parents, a lost friend, these are the things that can cut us to the bone.

But again, despite all of these things, we have to learn to be happy.

It's important to realize that happiness isn't something that is given to us. It isn't something we happen to bump into. It isn't something God or our spouse or our parents owe us. Happiness, like most important lessons in life, is something we have to *learn.*

And in this, as in everything, the Lord is our perfect example.

One of my favorite stories in the scriptures is found in the Pearl of Great Price. Moses tells this wonderful account of Enoch, who had a face-to-face discussion with God. As part of this revelation he was shown an astounding vision.

"Enoch beheld, and lo, all the nations of the earth were before him;

"And there came generation upon generation; and Enoch was high and lifted up, even in the bosom of the Father, and of the Son of Man; and behold, the power of Satan was upon all the face of the earth.

"And he saw angels descending out of heaven; and he heard a loud voice saying: Wo, wo be unto the inhabitants of the earth.

"And he beheld Satan; and he had a great chain in his hand, and it veiled the whole face of the earth with darkness; and he looked up and laughed, and his angels rejoiced. . . .

"And it came to pass that the God of heaven looked upon the residue of the people, and he wept; and Enoch bore record of it, saying: How is it that the heavens weep, and shed forth their tears as the rain upon the mountains?

"And Enoch said unto the Lord: How is it that thou canst weep, seeing thou art holy, and from all eternity to all eternity?" (Moses 7:23–26, 28–29).

Think about this. Enoch was shown all the nations of the earth, from the beginning to the end. Then, at the conclusion of that indescribable vision, he turned and was amazed to see that God was weeping. That puzzled him—and scared him just a little bit, I think. He knew who God was. He had seen His perfection and creations. And so Enoch asked God, "How is it thou canst weep?"

God answered by reminding Enoch that His children, His own offspring, had rejected Him:

"The Lord said unto Enoch: Behold these thy brethren ... in the day I created them; and in the Garden of Eden, gave I unto man his agency;

"And unto thy brethren have I said, and also given commandment, that they should love one another, and that they should choose me, their Father; but behold, they are without affection, and they hate their own blood" (Moses 7:32–33).

More, God knew His rebellious children were going to have to suffer for their sins. "Satan shall be their father, and misery shall be their doom; and the whole heavens shall weep over them, even all the workmanship of mine hands; wherefore should not the heavens weep, seeing these shall suffer?" (Moses 7:37).

As I read this, I get a sense of God's compassion and suffering for His children, His empathy and caring, even to the point of shedding tears.

But wait a minute ...

Isn't God supposed to be perfectly happy? What's this about sadness? What's this about tears? What happened to perfect joy?

Think about it. We know the heavens wept when Lucifer and his followers were cast out. Christ was angry at the moneychangers. He was a man of sorrows, with body, parts, and passion. He was disappointed with His followers from time to time, and at one time even "sore amazed" at His own suffering (Mark 14:33). These are not ungodly emotions. And if even Jesus and Heavenly Father feel those seemingly very human emotions from time to time, how could we possibly expect that we could live in this mortal world and not feel them as well? It is part of our existence. It seems to be an eternal part. And part of learning to be like our Father is learning to experience these emotions without letting them overtake us, without letting them define us or become the larger part of our lives.

We all feel discouraged. We all feel weary, frightened, amazed at our suffering, sad, lonely, maybe all of these things. It is unrealistic to think our lives will be devoid of such emotions. Life is a mix. We can accept that. It is not a bad thing.

Yet the foundational statement that we began this discussion with is still true: Men are, that they might have joy. Joy is *always* possible. Satan would have us not believe that. He would have us focus only on the disappointments in our lives.

I know we can be happy. But how can that be done?

BUT NO ONE
EVER TOLD ME LIFE
COULD BE SO . . .

"OKAY," YOU SAY, "SO THE PLAN was designed for us to learn to be happy. I guess I can accept that."

But the problem is—and this is a huge problem—*the enemy knows this too!*

Just like God knows us, Satan and his angels remember us as well. We fought them. We hurt them. We helped to defeat them and cast them out from the premortal world. And the veil that has been placed over our eyes may not have been placed over theirs. They may remember you and me. They want to destroy us. Lucifer wants to steal our happiness as much as he wants anything.

And because Satan strives to destroy us, *sometimes life can be hard!*

"What!" we say. "I never bargained for hard!"

No one ever told me the world would be so sinful.

No one ever told me one of my kids would turn out to be a complete conehead and wander off into la-la-land.

No one ever told me that marriage would be such a challenge.

No one told me that one of my children would be diagnosed with cancer, or that my mother would die, or my husband's business would fail and I'd have to go back to work, or my wife would leave me, or that . . .

The list goes on and on.

No one told us that life would sometimes be hard. But then, of course they did. We knew that before we agreed to come here. And still we were willing—not even just willing, we were *excited*—about the prospect of coming down here to earth.

Unfortunately, knowing that in our heads doesn't make the pain entirely go away when we are hurting in our hearts.

But think about this point: Lucifer knows our potential. He understands something about our missions and purposes in life. He knows we have been reserved to come forth in the latter days to help build the Lord's kingdom in preparation for His coming. And he will do *anything* to stop us. He will do everything he can to take away our joy.

But Heavenly Father will not desert us. Despite Lucifer's direct challenges, God will provide a way.

Elder Richard G. Scott taught something that helps me understand this: "The challenges you face, the growth experiences you encounter, are intended to be temporary scenes played out on the stage of a life of continuing peace and happiness. Sadness, heartache, and disappointments are events in life. It is not intended that they be the substance of life. I do not minimize how hard some of these events can be. When the lesson you are to learn is very important, trials can extend over a long period of time, but they should not be allowed to become the confining focus of every-thing you do. . . . That perspective keeps challenges confined to their proper place—stepping-stones to further growth and attainment" ("The Atonement Can Secure Your Peace and Happiness," *Ensign,* November 2006, 41).

There is another interesting story, also found in the book of Moses, that has helped me keep the perspective Elder Scott speaks about.

The first chapter of Moses begins, much like the story of Enoch, with a description of a meeting between Moses and God: "And he saw God face to face, and he talked with him, and the glory of God was upon Moses; therefore Moses could endure his presence" (Moses 1:2).

God began the conversation by reminding Moses of who He (God) really was: "Behold, I am the Lord God Almighty, and Endless is my name; for I am without beginning of days or end of years; and is not this endless?" (Moses 1:3).

In the next few verses, God attempted in various ways to help Moses begin to understand His incomprehensible glory: "I will show thee the workmanship of mine hands; but not all, for my works are without end, and also my words, for they never cease. Wherefore, no man can behold all my works, except he behold all my glory . . ." (Moses 1:4–5).

So Moses was shown "the world upon which he was created . . . and the ends thereof, and all the children of men which are, and which were created." Then, at the end of that amazing vision, Moses "said unto himself: Now, for this cause I know that man is nothing, which thing I never had supposed" (Moses 1:8, 10).

There it is, right in the scriptures. *Man is nothing, which thing I never had supposed.*

Sometimes I feel that way. Man is nothing. I am nothing. In the big scheme of things, in the entire operation and running of this entire universe, in the management of the affairs of all men, I don't amount to much. I don't like to think about it, but there it is. Even Moses had to admit it. Man is nothing. Why, then, should we wonder if God overlooks our pleadings from time to time? After all, He's got a lot of things to do.

But do you really think that was the lesson God intended for Moses to take away from this encounter? Is that really the lesson to be taught here?

I don't see how it could be! In fact, I think this sense of futility is exactly the opposite of what Moses was supposed to feel.

Yet that is what it says.

But look at the footnote to this scripture (10b). Something important is waiting there. Look down and you'll see this verse doesn't refer to man, but to mortality.

Man is nothing?

No, no, no. *Mortality* is nothing.

This life, the challenges we face here, the few times we suffer, the trials the Lord may give us in order that we might learn, all of these are nothing when compared to the eternities of time. They are mere fractions of a second when compared to the promise of eternal life.

And consider this critical point: In the midst of this conversation, while God is teaching Moses of His eternal majesty and indescribable power, He takes the time to remind Moses of a very important truth. "Behold, thou art my son," He says to him (Moses 1:4).

Behold, thou art my son! Can you feel that? Can we begin to understand what God is trying to convey in these few simple sentences? "I am the Lord God Almighty. Endless is my name. My works are without end. And you, Moses, *are my son!*"

If the seeds of eternity can be inherited—and they must be—how much power is there in this statement! *"I am the Lord God Almighty. And you are my son."*

Moses had just been told that he was God's son. He had been told that God had a great work for him to do. Through the power of the Spirit, he *knew and understood the plan.* After being shown the eternities of the universe, he also understood how quickly this all would pass.

Sometimes we think that this life, with all its challenges, is all we have. Sometimes we think these few moments in mortality are all we will ever be, all we will ever experience, and that the pinnacle of our happiness comes in only those pieces we find here.

Man is nothing?

No.

Mortality is nothing. Everything we are called upon to endure here shall pass.

The God of Heaven is our Father. Surely there is hope, then, for all His children as they struggle for a short time in this world.

We all know that we live in spiritually dangerous and perilous times. We know the challenges to our children. We all are aware of the forces of darkness that surround us. Sometimes we may think we are the first to feel this way, or that our challenges are unique.

Seven thousand years of history suggest this isn't true.

We aren't the first ones to wonder at our trials. We're not the first to feel overcome by the challenges in life. I believe the human experience, from the days of Adam through the ages and down to our day, is, at its essence, very much the same. The common thread of human experience passes through all times. Our challenges may be different, but our lives are basically more similar than we sometimes suppose.

We are born. We live. We laugh. Sometimes we cry.

It may not matter as much as we think what circumstances we are born into. Regardless of the time, place, or condition in which we find ourselves, the yearnings are much the same. We have challenges. We feel pain and triumph; we suffer and learn. We experience joy and disappointments, fear and temptations, happiness and love. And at the end of it all, we have to decide what we really believe and who we want to be.

One of my favorite songs in our hymnbook is "Be Still, My Soul" (*Hymns,* no. 124). For me, this hymn seems to capture many of the emotions that I feel regarding the challenges in life. It's interesting to see from the footnote at the bottom of the page that the words were written by Katharina von Schlegel, a woman who lived more than 300 years ago.

A woman living in medieval Europe. How much do I have in common with her life? How much could she relate to my life here in modern-day America? We come from very different worlds.

We live in very different times. Yet her ponderings on the challenges in life are similar to mine.

Times change, but people don't. That's been true from the very beginning. And so it is that a woman living so many years ago could write something that so many of us can still relate to today.

These things, then, are true:

- We were sent here to be happy.
- Lucifer would steal our happiness if we let him.
- The challenges of mortality, when compared with the wonders of eternity, are nothing.
- Though we may live in chaotic and tempting times, the entire human family has also struggled in every era.
- And just as God did for them, He will prepare a way to see us through.

With these truths in place, I think we can ask: Are there things we can do to reorient our lives in order to achieve greater joy and happiness?

REEVALUATING
OUR EXPECTATIONS

I HAVE COME TO BELIEVE that one of the first keys in finding greater joy is understanding the occasional need to reevaluate our expectations. Let me illustrate with a personal example.

A few days after I graduated from college, I sat down late one night and made a list of things I wanted to accomplish in my life. The list was pretty long and ran the gamut of ideas and goals. Some of these ideas were really, *really* important. I think the first thing on my list was that I wanted to fly upside down at 30,000 feet while going super-sonic. I've done that, and I have to tell you I pretty much consider my life complete now.

But there were other things I wrote down, too: have a family, stay temple worthy, do something meaningful. Some of the things I wrote were personal, some were trivial, some were important. I've kept that list through all these years. I don't refer to it very often. It's not like it has become my road map in life—it simply hasn't—but I like to keep it as a reminder and pull it out from time to time.

Do you think I've been able to accomplish everything on my list? Do you think my life has turned out the way I planned it?

I can promise you it hasn't.

Do you think I have never experienced disappointment or failure?

I can promise you I have.

I think many of us have such a list. Even if it's just a mental list, many of us keep an inventory of expectations that we use to measure the happiness or success of our lives.

And for almost all of us, these lists are painfully unrealistic.

Not long ago, I read of a survey that indicated the unhappiest group of people in the world (not just the United States) were people approaching middle age. Far and away, the main reason listed as the cause of their unhappiness was the fact that many of them realized they weren't going to accomplish most of their goals in life.

Let's pretend for a moment that you are eighteen again. (Now, I know you may be thinking, "No, please, don't make me go back and do it all again!" but this is just pretend, okay?) Just for a minute, let's pretend that you could go back and do what I did, write down a list of things you wanted to accomplish in your life. I suppose for most of us this list would include such things as:

- Having a family
- Having our children remain active in the Church
- Marrying a spouse who remained faithful to his or her testimony
- Having enough faith to see us through the hard times
- Having money (maybe even a lot of money!)
- Having opportunities to travel
- Enjoying good health

- Having a great relationship with our
  parents
- Having a successful career
- Accomplishing something worthwhile or
  memorable with our lives

The problem, of course, is that we tend to measure our lives by these expectations. But if you are like me, you can look upon some area of your life and realize it hasn't turned out the way you planned. All of us are like that. And measuring our happiness with an unrealistic yardstick is guaranteed to bring frustration and disappointment.

Now, I want to be very careful here. I don't mean to say that we shouldn't set high goals or strive for excellence, whether in our faith, family, community, or career. It is great to strive toward a worthy goal. The only thing I'm trying to warn about is that life may throw us a curveball. We need to be prepared for that. And if the curveballs in life happen to shatter a couple of windows, sometimes it's helpful to remember that that happens to everyone. Few of us live charmed lives. All of us have trials and disappointments. No one is able to accomplish every goal. And maintaining a healthy expectation is essential in finding true joy.

Are there relationships within your family that are not perfect? Do you struggle from time to time in your marriage? Have some of your children made foolish decisions? Do you struggle financially to make ends meet? Have you struggled with health or weight or faith or whatever?

Join the club.

We've all experienced trials like those. Each and every one of us. They are part of life.

Which is why it's so important that we redefine our expectations in order to accept these occasional pangs of disappointment. Learning to measure our joy with a realistic yardstick is critical to finding peace.

DEMANDING PERFECT WATER

WHEN I WAS A YOUNG LIEUTENANT, right after I graduated from pilot training, the Air Force sent me through a series of survival schools, the purpose of which was to teach me how to survive if I ever had to eject from my aircraft. These survival courses taught me how to live off the land (or in the water if I had to eject over the ocean), how to avoid enemy capture if I ejected behind enemy lines, and finally, how to survive in a prisoner of war camp. At one point I found myself going through desert survival training. As part of this course, I had to survive in the desert, living off what I could find, including water.

Several days into this training, I was so hot and tired and thirsty I thought I was going to die.

But instead of lying down and whining (which was what I felt like doing), I did what they had taught me to do. Finding an old streambed, I searched out some vegetation, then started digging in the sand. I dug and dug until I couldn't reach down any farther. Then, exhausted, I rolled up in my jacket and fell asleep. Overnight, a couple of inches of water seeped into my hole. When I woke up in the morning and saw that water, I thought it was the most beautiful thing I had ever seen. It was dirty and full of bugs and sand, but I didn't care. I knew it was enough to quench my thirst. I knew it was enough to keep me alive.

Our lives, like this water, may not be perfect. They may be a little gritty and have an occasional bug or mouthful of dirt. And if that's the case, we have two choices. We can go to God and demand that He sweep His hand across our lives and make them perfect. We can insist on drinking only the bottled water of life, then get angry or upset if we don't get what we want. Or we can ask ourselves, "Is the water I've been given enough? Yes, it may be dirty, but is it enough? Though my life may not be perfect, are the blessings I've been given enough to sustain me?"

There will be times in our lives—many times—when we will drink water that is cool and clean and pure. And during those times, we will drink in joy.

But there are other times when the Lord will ask us to endure, when the water of life may contain a little grit and sand. If we approach those times with the right perspective and appreciation, I think we will see that in almost every case, the water He gives us is enough. Even in the most challenging times we can live, if not in perfect happiness, then in perfect peace. And sometimes peace is all we need.

I know a woman who has had a very difficult life. Her father died young and her mother passed her around among various family members. In several of these situations, she was horribly abused. To put it mildly, she didn't have the light of the gospel in her life. Then, when she was twelve years old, her younger brother, the only person in her life who she really cared about and who really cared about her, was violently killed.

She remembers weeping and cursing God while wondering, "What have I done to make you quit loving me?"

I testify to you that such a conclusion isn't true. And she has learned that now. As difficult as this young woman's childhood was, she has learned the most important lesson in this life: God does love her. He always did. He always will. He loves us all. She knows that now.

Despite every challenge in her life—and there were many significant ones—she has learned to live a life of joy. I sometimes think of her and ask myself, "If she can do that, then can't I learn to do that too?"

As we look at our occasionally broken dreams or shattered expectations, sometimes I think it helps to ask ourselves, "Maybe I don't have everything, and maybe my life isn't perfect, but has God blessed me with enough to still be happy?" I think if we were really to consider this question, the answer would nearly always be yes.

OUR JOURNEY THROUGH THE WILDERNESS

THERE'S A GREAT PARALLEL in the Book of Mormon to our journey through life. I'm talking about Lehi's journey into the wilderness. I mean, look at these guys. It's pretty clear from the record that, in some ways, they were making it up as they went along.

Sometimes God will allow us to do that, you know. Even when we're on His errand, He'll make us figure it out.

It would have been so easy for Heavenly Father to send an angel down to talk to Lehi and explain it all to him. "Okay, you're heading out to a new land. You're going to be the father of an entire nation. Pretty heady stuff here, you know, so grab a pencil and take some notes on this. First, you'll need the

Brass Plates. Really important. Put a star by that one. Got to get the plates before you head off into the wilderness. Laban is going to fight you on this one, but don't worry about that, I'll tell you what to do about him later on. Next, you need wives for your sons. Ishmael's family will do. And lots of metal bows, okay? That's a big one. Take extra metal bows. Don't worry about the reason, you'll find out later on ..."

Wouldn't it have been nice (and *so* much easier) if God had sat down with Lehi and Nephi and told them everything they needed to make their journey into the wilderness a complete success?

But He didn't. Even though Lehi was His prophet, He made him figure some of these things out. We see the same thing with other prophets. The more I understand the challenges faced by the Prophet Joseph Smith, the more I see the same pattern in his life. He was a young man, barely more than a child, and yet Heavenly Father respected him enough to honor his intelligence and agency, allowing him to learn the lessons from figuring it out as he went along, allowing him the experience of making mistakes. To me, it's almost like God says, "Don't worry too much about how you're going to do it or about making mistakes along the way. I am God. I control the very heavens. I can help you. Do the best you can, seek my counsel, but don't be too afraid. Remember, you can't make a mistake that I can't fix."

So out into the wilderness Lehi and his family go. It's a long trip. They're hot and tired, maybe a little hungry. They camp for a couple of days. *"Hey, we need the plates!"* Okay, head on back to Jerusalem. Ask Laban for the plates. He laughs and then gets angry. They try to buy them. He steals their gold and sends his men to kill them. Finally they get the plates. Head on back into the wilderness. Camp a couple of days. *"Hey, we need some wives!"* (Notice Laman and Lemuel were finally given a commandment they didn't murmur about.) Okay, hike on back to Jerusalem. Got the plates, got the wives, start the journey through the wilderness. Hungry. Thirsty. Hot and cold. Hunting. Hunting. Broke the bow. *"Dang it! Anyone got another bow? What! Are you telling me we left Jerusalem without a stash of metal bows! Oh man, we're going to die!"*

Our journey through life is like this. We can't prepare for everything. We scramble to make things work, but no one travels through the wilderness of life in a limousine. And if you think some people do, you're wrong. Elder Neal A. Maxwell said there is far more equity in our challenges than we may realize.

We all get discouraged. Sariah got discouraged and fearful for her children. For a moment there, she lost her faith, "for she truly had mourned because of us. For she had supposed that we had perished in the wilderness; and she also had complained against my father, telling him that he was a visionary man; saying: Behold thou hast led us forth from the land of our inheritance, and my sons are no more, and we perish in the wilderness. And after this manner of language had my mother complained against my father" (1 Nephi 5:1–3).

Sariah, strong and faithful as she was, mother of an entire nation, struggled with the challenges the Lord required of her. And she wasn't the only

one. Lehi, her husband and the prophet, got discouraged and fearful over providing food for his
family. Even he wavered in his faith for a short
time, as described by Nephi:

"And after I did break my bow, behold, my
brethren were angry with me because of the loss of
my bow, for we did obtain no food.

"And it came to pass that we did return without food to our families, and being much fatigued,
because of their journeying, they did suffer much
for the want of food.

"And it came to pass that Laman and Lemuel
and the sons of Ishmael did begin to murmur
exceedingly, because of their sufferings and afflictions in the wilderness; and *also my father began to murmur against the Lord his God*" (1 Nephi 16:18–20;
emphasis added).

The problem was, they didn't realize their journey through the wilderness would be so hard. They
didn't realize it would be so long. I don't think we
can imagine how difficult it was for them; I go
camping for two days and I'm done. I want a
shower. I want a microwave oven and a soft bed.

Now, imagine camping with your children for *eight years,* entirely dependent for your food and water on what you can find in the wilderness. I have flown over this area. Even the Saudis call it the Empty Quarter; there is simply nothing there. And after years of this, Laman and Lemuel were starting to wonder. So they went to Nephi to make their point. "We have wandered in the wilderness for these many years; and our women have toiled, being big with child; and they have borne children in the wilderness and suffered all things, save it were death; and it would have been better that they had died before they came out of Jerusalem than to have suffered these afflictions. Behold, these many years we have suffered in the wilderness, which time we might have enjoyed our possessions and the land of our inheritance; yea, and we might have been happy" (1 Nephi 17:20–21).

In essence, they were saying, "We could have been a lot happier if we didn't have to make this journey and if it wasn't always so hard!"

Maybe we all can relate to this on a certain level. Am I the only one who wonders about my journey in the wilderness? Am I the only one who sometimes asks the Lord, Why? Why does the journey have to be so long, so hard, so full of trials?

Is it wrong to wonder sometimes why it has to be this way?

But Nephi gave a brilliant answer. He summed up the reason perfectly. He talked about the children of Israel as they wandered for forty years in the desert, being fed manna, being led by the light of the Lord, and finally crossing over the River Jordan, finally making it home to the promised land. Then Nephi answered his brothers' objection by saying, "And after they had crossed the river Jordan he did make them mighty" (1 Nephi 17:32). Mighty enough to conquer the land. Mighty enough to destroy the enemies they were to find there.

Mighty enough to find success in all their doings.

Isn't that what we want?

All of us want to make it home to our Father in Heaven. But don't you also want to be a mighty person, a mighty servant, a mighty family? And there's only one way to do that. We have to make our own journey in the wilderness. We have to face our trials and challenges. We have to pay the price.

But the Lord gives us this amazing promise: "And I will also be your light in the wilderness; and I will prepare the way before you, if it so be that ye shall keep my commandments; wherefore, inasmuch as ye shall keep my commandments ye shall be led towards the promised land; and ye shall know that it is by me that ye are led. Yea … after ye have arrived in the promised land, ye shall know that I, the Lord, am God" (1 Nephi 17:13–14).

I have come to understand that there is great joy in becoming mighty! Even joy in the battle. And is there anything better than being victors in the war we find ourselves engaged in this day?

TRUE GIFTS

ONE OF THE THINGS I have thought and spoken about often is the premortal world. I just think there was so much that happened there, so many things we learned and were taught that were designed to prepare us for our time here on earth. I believe there was far more loving and personal instruction from our Heavenly Father than we can imagine.

We had someone leave our office once to take a position with another company. Before he left, we had a little party for him and presented him with several gifts. I wonder if it was like that before we came to earth. Did we have a little going-away party, a little *bon voyage,* to send us on our way? If we didn't, we certainly should have. I mean, come on, we're sitting there in heaven; surely we were always looking for reasons to have a party. So let's pretend that we did, and that Heavenly Father gave us a couple of really special gifts before we came down here to earth. I can picture it: We go running over, so excited. Heavenly Father is going to give us some of the gifts we can use down on earth. We run to this pile of gifts and start to tear them open.

Maybe one of the gifts we opened said something like this: *I give you the gift of a loving family on earth.*

Wow. That's a good one! A loving family. I mean, we know how important that is. And if we were to look around, we could all see some really deserving people who weren't given this special gift.

We tear into another present, throwing paper and ribbons aside. Opening it up, maybe we read something like this: *I give you the gift of a healthy body.*

Cool. Love that. A healthy body. Those among us who struggle with poor health maybe appreciate this great gift more than anyone else.

Another gift. We tear it open. *I give you the blessings of the gospel in your life.*

This one really made us jump up and down. The blessings of the gospel! The whole thing! You're talking temples and priesthood blessings and prophets and scriptures, all of the things that make our lives so much easier and more meaningful down here on earth.

There were other gifts that Heavenly Father gave us. Piles of them. Some were huge. A couple were small. But all of them were special gifts from Him.

But I wonder . . . did we open every one? Or were there a few gifts we reached for and Heavenly Father put His hand on them and held them back. "These are very special gifts," He told us. "I'd like you to open these gifts later on."

So we left them on the table, still unopened, wondering what they were.

But we didn't worry too much about it, *because we trusted Him.* And He had given us so many beautiful gifts already.

So let's imagine that we left a couple of these gifts on the table, and we'll come back to talk about them later on.

MY FIRST GIFT

I HAVE TO TELL YOU a personal story about one of the special gifts God saved for me. In fact, I'm going to tell you two personal stories. In doing so, I hope you will forgive me: I don't want to be self-absorbed, and I certainly don't mean to suggest that I have experienced any greater challenges in life than you have. I recognize that many of Heavenly Father's children have taken on tremendous burdens and carry them with extraordinary grace. When you hear about my tales of woe, you might think, "What? That's it? What a baby!" But, just like I don't think it's a good idea to compare our blessings in life, I don't think it's a good idea to compare our trials either. Still, if experience is the master teacher—and in many ways it is—over the past few years I've been taught a thing or two.

I am the president and owner of my own business. As is true of a lot of business owners, my personal finances are intricately intertwined with those of my business. At one time, two of the most senior and trusted people in my company did some very bad things. They engaged in greedy and dishonest practices, and by the time we found out, it was far too late. The things they did had a huge impact on our company. Overnight, our revenues were cut by almost 45 percent. The company was brought to the brink of financial ruin.

There are special burdens that men carry because we have the primary responsibility of providing for our families, and, for some, this is a constant stress and worry. "By the sweat of thy face shalt thou eat bread, until thou shalt return unto the ground," we are taught (Moses 4:25). And I have to tell you, for me this was a gut-wrenching experience. For almost two years, it was all I ever thought about. It was like a pit inside my stomach every minute of the day. I remember going for walks alone, late at night, and wondering, *Why? What was I supposed to do?* And, I'll be honest, there were times when I thought, "Okay, Heavenly Father, you've driven me to my knees. I don't know what to do now. I know I'm supposed to learn something from this experience, but haven't I learned it yet?"

One evening I found myself driving to the temple. I wasn't seeking any particular inspiration, I was just fulfilling a stake temple assignment. And as I was driving, these are some of the thoughts I had: "Okay, Chris, you're probably going to lose the company. And if you do, you're going to lose your home." Now, I love my house, it's a beautiful home, but we had lived in enough places while we were in the Air Force that I knew we could live almost anywhere and be happy. So that wasn't the thing that bothered me. The thing that really made me feel bad was worrying about my younger children. I knew they weren't going to understand the circumstances of this move. They weren't going to understand why we had to sell our home and move into a much smaller home, maybe even an apartment.

They weren't going to understand why they had to leave their friends and start over in a new ward or school. I knew that the circumstances of such a move were going to scare them.

As I wrestled with this gut-wrenching fear, suddenly, out of nowhere, a soft and peaceful feeling settled over my soul. At that moment, the Spirit very clearly said to me, *"Chris, even if all of this happens, you and your family can still be happy."*

I thought about it, immediately understanding this was true.

"Chris, even if all of this happens, you and your family can still be happy."

It was at this point that I got to open one of those special presents we talked about before, one of those gifts God had chosen for me up in heaven. I opened it up, and this is what it said:

I give you the gift of hope for the future.

And that is what this experience has done for me. I have such peace and hope about my future now. We didn't end up losing the house, but I realize that it doesn't matter what home we live in, how much money we have, what kind of car we drive—as long as we have our faith, we can still be happy. If I were to lose all of those earthly possessions that I was so worried about, I might mope around for a few weeks, feeling sorry for myself, but then I would rebuild. I know now, and really believe, that no matter what happens around me, as long as my family and I are faithful, we can still be happy.

Really understanding this, I can look to the future without any fear, regardless of the physical circumstances around me. This very difficult time turned out to be a great gift. The peace that has come through this promise of hope has made it much easier for me to be happy now.

My Second Gift

SOME TIME AGO we had a medical crisis in my family, to the point where we thought we might lose one of my children. This went on for about five months, during which time my son suffered greatly. He was in pain. He lost a great deal of weight. He couldn't sleep because of the suffering he was experiencing. Every week this child grew sicker and sicker and there was nothing the doctors could do either to help him get better or to relieve his suffering.

I remember walking into his bedroom one morning to pick up his laundry and seeing that all his clothes were speckled with blood from the sores that had spread across his body. All night long he would walk around the house because it was so painful to sit or lie down. I remember taking him for a car ride in the middle of the night hoping that, as it sometimes happens with a child in a car seat, it might help him relax or feel a little better. My poor wife spent many nights staying up with him so that he wasn't alone. Through this experience she remarked that she was beginning to understand why Jesus had asked His disciples to stay awake and watch and pray with Him as He suffered in Gethsemane.

I can't tell you how difficult it was, as a parent, to watch my son suffer and not be able to help him or know what was going to happen. Sometimes in my prayers I would just cry. It was so painful. And then I'd feel guilty, crying for my own pain. I would almost yell at myself. "What are you doing, crying for yourself! You should be praying and crying for *him!*" But I always was. I shared his pain. I shared his discouragement and discomfort. I shared it all.

Then I remembered reading in *Jesus the Christ* where Elder James E. Talmage talked about examples in the Gospels where parents went to Jesus asking Him to ease the suffering of their children, but they asked in the first person, as if they were pleading for themselves. "Have compassion on us, and help us," they said (Mark 9:22), even though it was their children who were suffering. The Canaanite woman pled with Jesus to have mercy on her, though it was her daughter who was afflicted; the centurion pled for his servant as if he were pleading for himself.

And that's when I realized that exercising faith on behalf of others means taking on their suffering as if it were our own. I had taken on my son's suffering. In my mind and heart, we were the same. And I realized that when we are able to take on another's suffering in this way, when we are able to implore the Lord for another as if we were imploring for ourselves, with all of the same energy and emotion, that is when we are able to truly exercise faith on their behalf. That is when we are able to truly pray for them and make a difference.

It takes an incredible spiritual and emotional effort to do this. I think we only truly do it maybe a couple of times in our lives.

And yet, in Gethsemane, Christ did this and more for every single person on the earth. One by one, 125 billion times, He took on every person's suffering, exercising all of the physical, emotional, mental, and spiritual effort to take on that person's pain as if it were His own.

During this time in my life the Spirit constantly reminded me: *Everything you have been taught and believed is true. Christ lived. He is the Savior. That's the only thing that matters. Everything else will be okay.*

So it was that I was able to open another of those special gifts from Father in Heaven. And when I opened it up, this is what it said:

I give you the gift of compassion so that you might begin to understand the Atonement.

In some ways, this has become the most important and meaningful gift I have been given in this life. It has changed me in ways I can't even begin to explain. My son is fine now, but even if things had turned out differently, I would still retain this most precious gift of understanding.

As I consider some of these meaningful but difficult gifts that God has given me, I realize one very important thing: My life is richer now, deeper, my faith more complete, my joy more full. I am a better man. I am more willing to look at the long term, more patient, more optimistic, more inclined to faith.

Am I happier?

That's a very good question, especially in regard to our discussion here.

So I ask again. Am I happier now? Is my joy more full?

The answer is yes.

Joy is not the same as some momentary, giddy, teenage, jump-up-and-down-I'm-just-so-happy-I-could-die emotion. It is longer. Deeper. Far more meaningful. Far greater. *And we gain it only through testimony and life experience.* But the reward—the gift of joy that God is willing to give us—is always worth the price.

When I consider the great trials we experience in our lives, I love to remember what Elder Neal A. Maxwell once said: "I testify that in eloquent example He partook voluntarily of the bitter cup in the awful, but for Him avoidable, Atonement;

we must, therefore, drink from our tiny cups. I thank Him for likewise not interceding on our behalf, even when we pray in faith and reasonable righteousness for that which would not be right for us. Our glimpse of Gethsemane should teach us that all prayers are petitions! ... I testify that He and the Father are serious about stretching our souls in this second estate" ("Jesus of Nazareth, Savior and King," *Ensign,* December 2007, 47).

God will stretch us. But He will also bless us. And when we submit ourselves to His teaching, our lives become so much more meaningful, our joy more full.

THESE SPECIAL GIFTS ARE GIVEN WITH GREAT THOUGHT

N OT LONG AGO I was talking to a group down in California. As part of the presentation, I asked each of those sitting on the first few rows to write down on a little slip of paper the greatest challenge or trial they had experienced in their lives. We collected these slips in a paper bag and, later on in the presentation, I had a woman from the audience come up next to me on the stand. I asked her, "Think about the greatest challenge in your life. Then tell me, if you could, would you reach into this paper bag and trade that trial for one of these?"

She thought a moment then answered, "Yeah, I think I would."

"Why would you do that?"

She looked at the first row of people, most of whom appeared to be very happy, with great families and successful careers, then answered hopefully, "Maybe I'll get something easier."

Then something hit me, something I had never thought about before. It wasn't something I had planned on saying, but it might have been the most important thing I could have said to her at that point.

I asked her, "Tell me, would you reach into this bag and trade your trial for one of these if you knew the Savior was standing here right now, waiting and listening carefully for your answer?"

She thought for a long moment, then finally answered, "No, I guess I wouldn't."

Why not? Nothing had changed. Her problems were the same. The odds of reaching into the bag and pulling out an easier set of challenges hadn't changed.

But something was different. Something had changed her mind. And in that moment, both she and I were taught. The reason she wouldn't exchange her problems was because she realized that the Lord had chosen her trials for her. Her trials weren't some random event, some chance piece of paper drawn out of a sack. A loving Heavenly Father who knew her strengths and weaknesses had specifically selected the challenges she would encounter in her life.

That's true for all of us.

And when we come to see and really believe that our trials are actually and truly gifts from God, that there is goodness in the learning, that though it may be difficult, there is a pathway out, then we will be stronger and better and happier—much happier—for our challenges.

Once experience has taught us this, we expand our capacity to feel joy.

DARKNESS AND LIGHT

A FINAL THOUGHT.

I'll always remember one of my last flights in the Air Force. I took off around sunset in a high-performance jet and climbed very high. As I flew, the earth was laid out before me: the clouds, the mountains, the land and rivers and lakes. It was so beautiful. I remember thinking, *It just can't get any better than this.*

I leveled off and flew east. And as I did, the sun sank below the horizon behind me and it grew dark. And the darkness revealed the incredible array of stars that were over my head. I could see them perfectly. Believe me, you haven't seen the stars until you've seen them through a perfectly clear canopy at 43,000 feet. It seemed like there were billions of them. The Milky Way. The moon.

And I was reminded that the world, in all its beauty, is just the beginning. There is so much more. So much more beauty. So much more light. Galaxies and universes we can't even imagine. The wonder of eternity. That's why we all love to look at the night stars. There's something inside each of us that senses there is more life out there, more beauty and creations than we can imagine, God's mighty work and glory.

But we can't see any of that until it is dark.

Just like I couldn't begin to understand the Atonement until I had a significant period of darkness in my own life.

Just like I couldn't understand hope until I had faced my own fear.

It is in the darkness that we really see the light.

It is hard. But it is worth it. I know that is true. Even as everything around us seems to go dark in our troubled times, there is light there above us, far greater and more beautiful than anything we can ever see on earth. These are the gifts God will give us, if we are willing to pay the price.

And knowing this is one of the greatest elements of living a joyful life.

Through all the confusion and challenges around us, this much I know. Jesus Christ actually lived in Jerusalem. He lives now. He knows us, our names, our happiness, our trials. He hears our pleadings and doesn't stand idly by. I pray that we will remember why we're here, that occasional heartaches are a necessary but temporary part of life, that though it may be difficult, mortality with its challenges is nothing when compared with the eternal nature of our souls. I hope that we are able to establish realistic yardsticks by which to measure the success and happiness of our lives, that we will accept our dirty water when it is necessary, knowing it is enough. I pray that our journey through the wilderness will be guided and that we will recognize and appreciate the gifts of trials that God has chosen for us.

I pray we may all find the happiness God intends for us as we struggle in these last days to become more like Him.

I know that He will help us.

I hope you know that too.